RENT COLLECTION COURTYARD

Sculptures of Oppression and Revolt

FOREIGN LANGUAGES PRESS
PEKING 1970

First Edition   1968
Second Edition   1970

Printed in the People's Republic of China

QUOTATION FROM
CHAIRMAN MAO TSETUNG

The ruthless economic exploitation and political oppression of the peasants by the landlord class forced them into numerous uprisings against its rule. . . . It was the class struggles of the peasants, the peasant uprisings and peasant wars that constituted the real motive force of historical development in Chinese feudal society.

"The Chinese Revolution and
the Chinese Communist Party"

Foreword

This grand exhibition of life-size clay figures takes its setting from the former rent collection courtyard of Liu Wen-tsai, a landlord despot of Tayi County, Szechuan Province in southwestern China. It recreates a profound, vivid and truthful picture of the raging class struggle in old China's countryside.

Before liberation the people of Tayi suffered untold misery through the brutalities of the local despots and the oppressive taxes levied by the reactionary Kuomintang government. Only three or four per cent of the local population were landlords, yet they occupied almost four-fifths of the arable land, mercilessly exploiting and oppressing the peasants and driving them to a life worse than that of beasts of burden. The Tayi of pre-liberation times was typical in semi-colonial and semi-feudal old China.

Under the leadership of the Chinese Communist Party headed by the great leader Chairman Mao Tsetung, the Chinese people in 1949 threw off the rule of imperialism, feudalism and bureaucrat-capitalism and established the People's Republic of China. Since then the people of Tayi, like those in other parts of China, have been liberated; they have set out on the socialist road and have marched bravely forward in the socialist revolution and socialist construction.

The more than a hundred sculptured figures portraying the story of rent collection are the work of a group of revolutionary Chinese art workers who, following the path lit by invincible Mao Tsetung Thought, studied and applied Chairman Mao's works in a living way, completely immersed themselves in worker, peasant and soldier life, and gave full play to collective effort.

The sculptures — arranged in six scenes — angrily condemn the feudal landlord class in old China for its heinous crimes of ruthless exploitation and oppression of the peasants; they deeply reflect the fierce class struggle waged by hundreds of millions of Chinese peasants under the leadership of the Chinese Communist Party headed by the great leader Chairman Mao Tsetung, to overthrow the merciless rule of the feudal landlord class and capture power for the people.

Rent Collection Courtyard is a striking example of sculpture serving the workers, peasants and soldiers and socialism. It is a brilliant achievement of the Great Proletarian Cultural Revolution and a victory for great Mao Tsetung Thought.

Liu Wen-tsai's Private Kingdom

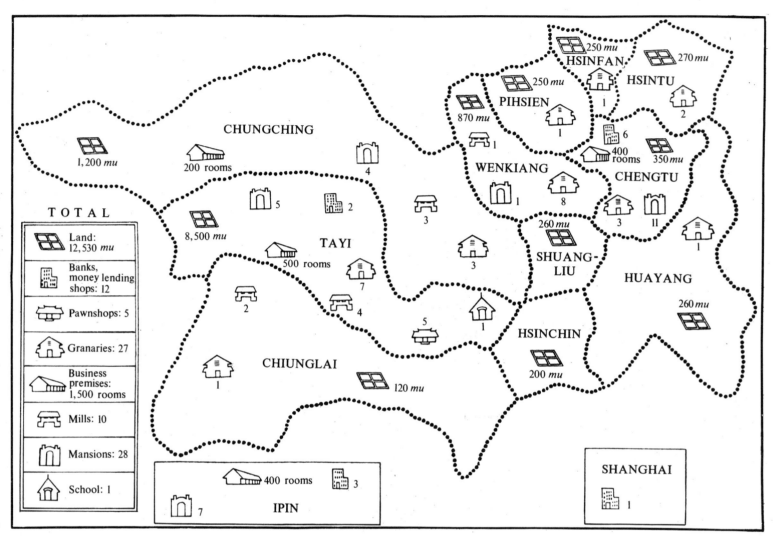

The tentacles of landlord Liu Wen-tsai of Tayi in Szechuan Province stretched out to more than a dozen counties and towns. But Liu was more than just a despotic landlord. He was also a Kuomintang warlord, a government official and a chieftain of a secret society. Altogether his clan seized more than 200,000 mu[1] of land. His family alone occupied over 12,000 mu, extorting an annual rent of 5,600,000 jin[2] of grain. Wielding his tyrannical power he engaged in blackmail, corruption, bribery, smuggling and in the traffic of drugs. Landlord Liu bled the people white.

---

[1] One mu is about one-sixth of an acre.
[2] One jin equals approximately 1.1 pounds.

The Manor-House of Crime

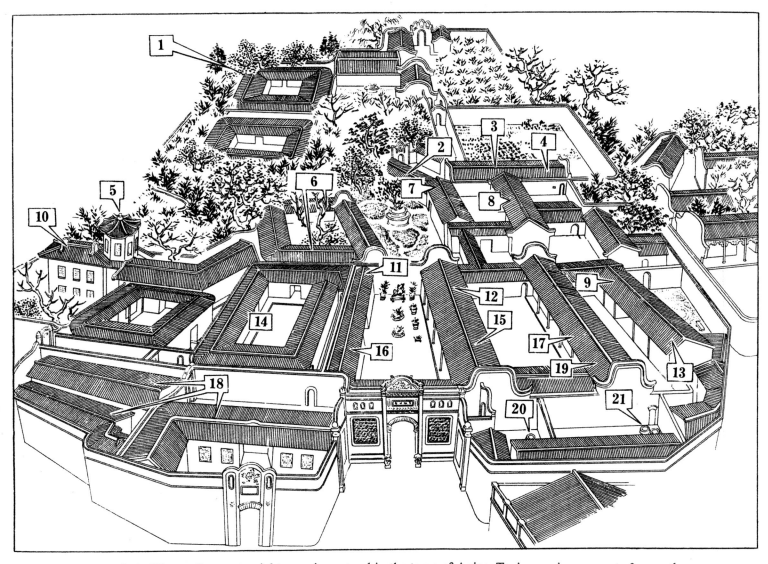

Two of Liu Wen-tsai's twenty-eight mansions stood in the town of Anjen, Tayi, covering an area of more than sixty *mu* of land. Their bricks were stained with the sweat and tears of the peasants, for Liu built them by seizing the land and houses of more than a hundred poor peasant families. After liberation these manor-houses were made into a museum which the Chinese people visit as a grim reminder of the past so that generation after generation will never forget class struggle. The clay figures are displayed in the rent collection courtyard in the northwest corner of one of these manor-houses.

1. Rent Collection Courtyard
2. Summer opium-smoking room
3. Granaries
4. Water dungeon
5. Tower of Joy
6. Storage-rooms
7. Hall of Pleasure
8. Buddhist prayer room
9. Third opium-smoking room
10. Boudoir
11. Counting house
12. Sitting-room (Chinese style)
13. Guest rooms for ladies
14. Servants' quarters
15. Sitting-room (Western style)
16. Reception room for sworn brothers of secret societies
17. Liu Wen-tsai's bedroom
18. Granaries
19. Second opium-smoking room
20. Servants' well
21. Master's well

The Rent Collection Courtyard

This courtyard, built especially for the collection of rent, is surrounded by a hundred-metre long corridor in which stand the clay figures. Hungry peasants had to use the back door to pay rent.

Instruments of Exploitation and Torture

Water dungeon.

Steel spring whips.

Measuring pecks.

The "trick" winnower.

Liu Wen-tsai used various criminal means to seize land from the peasants and force them to pay rent and debts. The peasants were locked in water dungeons, flogged with steel spring whips, buried alive and subjected to many other excruciating tortures and devilish cruelties. Above are some of the means used to exploit and oppress the peasants.

Part One

Tenants Pay Rent
—Their Harvest of Bitterness

The basic form of landlord exploitation is rent collection. Because of his widespread ownership of land Liu Wen-tsai placed a notice in the newspapers every year at the time of rent collection, announcing the date. No peasant was allowed to postpone payment, even if a death occurred in the family. Shortly after the autumn harvest, thousands of tenants would come to Liu's house to pay rent, bringing with them the bulk of their crops for which they had toiled throughout the year.

Under the cold gaze of the landlord's stooge, the poverty-stricken peasants trudge into the courtyard carrying the grain they have toiled so bitterly for.

With no family to help her this broken-hearted old widow cannot fully meet her debts. So she brings her last possession — a hen — to make up the difference.

An old man wheels in the grain he has reaped with his own blood and sweat.

A family with their heavy load of rent.

The crushing load of rent symbolizes the man-eating feudal system of exploitation.

Even a tottering, sick man has to drag in his rent on time.

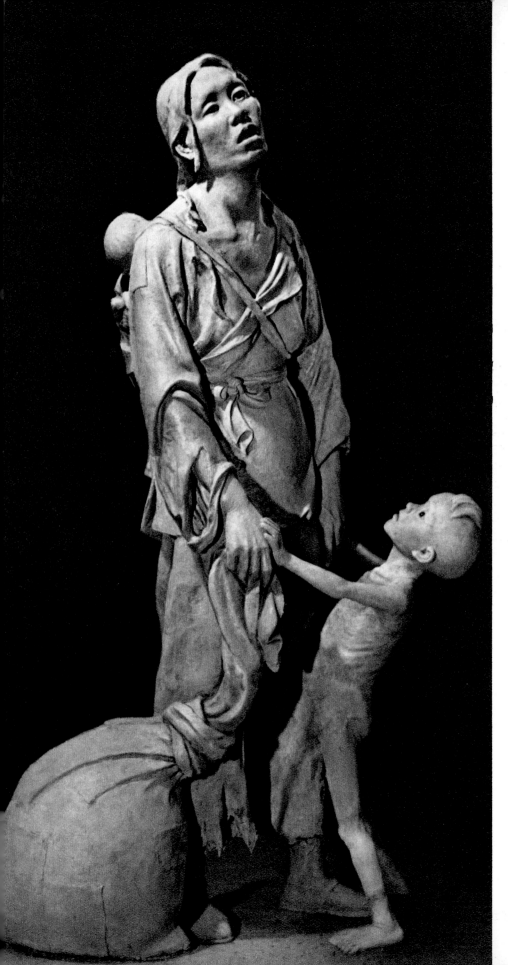

This exhausted woman with her children, all skin and bones, brings her last half bag of grain to pay the rent.

This starving old couple have to give their last bit of grain as rent.

We'll settle ac-
counts with you one
day, no matter how
vicious you are!

Part Two

Liu's Strong-arm Men Check the Grain

Liu Wen-tsai exploited the peasants in many criminal ways. His exploitation was particularly glaring during the payment of rent.

Liu's strong-arm men were always very exacting when they were checking the rent. If a thug did not like a single grain, he would say the whole lot was not up to standard and then curse and whip the peasant.

After the peasants' grain had been sifted, it would be put into a "trick" winnower where nearly one-third of the first grade grain would be blown away by a powerful fan and then collected by the landlord's men. As a result, many tenants were unable to pay their rent in full. Here the extortions of the landlord were nakedly revealed.

The thug's harsh demands cannot be met, so he kicks the old man to the ground, knocking his basket of grain over.

...She stiffens with anger at the thug's cruelty.

This old peasant is frantic with worry. He knows the same fate awaits him. How long can one stand by without doing something about it?

It is the peasants' blood and sweat that is thrown in and blown out.

This little girl has to stand on tiptoe to load the grain into the devouring winnower.

Not enough grain
to meet the rent.
The winnower has
played its trick.

The winnower groans and thuds and fear runs through the tenants.... Meanwhile, the little boy is whipped because he wants to take home some of the grain that has been blown out. And lashed too is the old man as he argues with the thug.

"This *is* good grain!" cries the old peasant.

Part Three

The "Bloody Mouth" of the Peck Measure

The peck measure Liu Wen-tsai used for measuring rent grain was bigger than the one used for loaning grain to the peasants, the difference being about one-third of a peck. Every year the landlord extorted over a million extra *jin* of grain by using the larger peck measure. "It makes us tremble to see the peck measure," said the peasants. "It looks like a big bloody mouth devouring our flesh and blood." Larger peck measures and fiendish thugs were criminal tools in the hands of the landlords for the ruthless oppression and exploitation of the peasants.

The "trick" winnower has reduced two full baskets of grain to one. With heavy hearts mother and daughter drag it to be measured.

The old peasant stares blankly at the peck measure under the thug's foot, wondering what he will say if the grain is too little. Will he be flogged if he says that's all he's got? If he promises to make up the difference, where will he get the grain?

Will her grain fill the peck measure?

The grain for which he has toiled the whole year will soon be added to Liu Wen-tsai's stores. But is it enough to satisfy the gaping peck measure?

What kind of a world is this?

How black-hearted
the landlord is!

After paying his rent the peasant carefully counts his tally sticks. The doubt torments him: will he ever be able to pay off his debts to the landlord?

Part Four

The Abacus That Ruins the Tenants

Liu Wen-tsai's outrageous rent ran as high as eighteen pecks for one *mu* of land. No deductions were ever allowed for floods, droughts or personal misfortunes.

The clicking of the landlord's abacus spelt bankruptcy for the tenants while the cold-blooded Liu indulged in debauchery and extravagance. Why did the peasants toil all the year round and still suffer from hunger and cold? Why were the landlords able to lead such a life of luxury without doing a solitary day's work? How unjust is the society of exploitation of man by man!

Fleeced by the "trick" winnower and then brutally knocked down. That is what happened to this old peasant. His "crime"? He refused to put his finger-print on a piece of paper certifying the sale of his son into the warlord army.

"You're a man-eating beast!" the peasant accuses.

Liu's hand tells beads while his heart is as enomous as a viper. How many peasants have been bankrupted by his steward's abacus?

A Kuomintang soldier and a secret society henchman lay hands on the old peasant's son as he rushes up to argue with landlord Liu.

The peasants burn with anger at the sight of the thugs' violence.

Her husband worked all his life like an animal for the landlord. Now he is dead. Yet she has not enough grain to clear off his debt...no money to pay for his coffin ... no comfort to give her fatherless child.

His hatred mounts, for the landlord not only extorts
rent but also pressgangs young men into the army.

The frightened child clings frantically to her angry grandmother.

His eyes are filled with the fury of revenge.

Class brothers, unite to settle the blood debts with the landlords!

Part Five

Forcing Payment

Besides ruthlessly exploiting the peasants, the landlords also oppressed them politically with the aid of their puppets: the Kuomintang village chiefs and policemen. The landlords used every cruel means to extort rent from the peasants. Those who failed to pay their rent in full were faced with inhuman torture and forced to sell their children. Families were broken up and men died for no cause.

In a society of exploitation and oppression there are many cases of barbarity and brutality like those perpetrated by Liu Wen-tsai. The following reflect the wrongs done to the peasants from generation to generation by the landlord class, the hatred they harboured and the tears and blood they shed.

A mother is torn from her child on the pretext of not having paid the rent so that Liu can drink fresh human milk every day.

Drought spells even deeper grief for this young woman and her mother-in-law. Because of it they cannot pay their rent. Now, the landlord has stripped them of their land and taken away the hard-earned deposit they put on it.

A blind man is forced to sell his grand-daughter as a bond-maid to Liu in place of the rent he cannot meet. In his left hand is the receipt for the girl he depended so much on.

There seems no end
to life's bitterness.

The rent collection courtyard is like a hell on earth as peasants who cannot pay their rent are locked away in underground or water dungeons. Here the body of one of the victims is being carried out.

Her rent is paid but her sack is empty. How can she keep alive without a single grain of rice left?

This mother grips the bars in hatred as her helpless children cry.

Liu orders the village chief and a policeman to ransack the homes of peasants and pressgang them if they cannot pay their rent. Another family is broken up as the father is dragged away and the mother is knocked to the ground.

Part Six

Seizing Power

Under the cruel exploitation and oppression of the landlords, the peasants, seething with bitter class hatred, rose in revolt. They got organized under the leadership of the Chinese Communist Party and carried on an unyielding armed struggle against the landlord class.

The Chinese People's Liberation Army liberated Szechuan in 1949 and, with the co-operation of the revolutionary masses, captured Liu Wen-tsai, thoroughly smashed the rule of the reactionary classes and established the new political power of the people. Under the wise leadership of the Chinese Communist Party headed by the great leader Chairman Mao Tsetung, the emancipated peasants, holding high the great red banner of Mao Tsetung Thought, determined to carry the proletarian revolution through to the end.

The landlord's reign of pitiless exploitation and oppression has aroused the peasants' deep vengeance and revolt.

"I'll destroy the landlord's den with my axe!"

With their carrying-poles they will smash the system of exploitation to bits.

Only by thoroughly demolishing the man-eating system can the working people be emancipated.

We will arm ourselves with weapons seized from the thugs!

Led by the Chinese Communist Party, the peasants, confident of victory, take up weapons and march off to the mountains to wage armed struggle and shatter the old world.

The young generation too will take up arms and make revolution, to completely tear down all the vicious "rent collection courtyards" in the world.

Let's go to the mountains
and join the guerrillas!

Follow forever the Chinese Communist Party and raise high the red flag of revolution.

If the army and the people are united as one, who in the world can match them?

The workers and peasants rise in their millions to rebel and capture the landlord Liu Wen-tsai.

"Political power grows out of the barrel of a gun." Red political power will be handed down from generation to generation.

Sailing the seas depends on the helmsman, making revolution depends on Mao Tsetung Thought.

收租院泥塑群像

*

外文出版社出版（北京）
1968年（12开）第一版
1970年第二版
编号：（英）8050—952
00170
85—E—107P